Make Today An Affirmations

Make Today Amazing Workbook of Affirmations: Bullet Journal, Food Diary, Recipe Notebook, Planner, To Do List, Scrapbook, Academic Notepad.

Alan Haynes

Copyright © 2018

All rights reserved. Without limiting rights under the copyright reserved above, no part of this publication may be reproduced, stored, introduced into a retrieval system, distributed or transmitted in any form or by any means, including without limitation photocopying, recording, or other electronic or mechanical methods, without the prior written permission of the publisher, except in the case of brief quotations embodied in critical reviews and certain other non-commercial uses permitted by copyright law.

The scanning, uploading, and/or distribution of this document via the internet or via any other means without the permission of the publisher is illegal and is punishable by law. Please purchase only authorized editions and do not participate in or encourage electronic piracy of copyrightable materials.

Introduction

Welcome to this affirmations workbook.

We have collated a set of positive affirmations, all aimed at inspiring and lifting your mood in order to help bring the best out of you. Through our research and testing, we discovered how the mind absorbs and applies information.

Reading and repeating positive affirmations are a great way to support your sub-conscious mind. As a result, you will notice significant shifts within yourself, for the better.

You are also welcome to use this workbook as a diary, notepad, scrap book, daily/monthly planner, photo album, ideas & brainstorming pad, a Bullet Journal, a To-Do List – or even a record log for anything that you want to keep track and details of. Use it in a way that best serves you – be creative with it.

Life mastery is the goal. We also encourage users to repeat all of the affirmations found within, at least ten times, first thing in the morning and just before bed time. We have found this to contribute towards the development of an increased positive outlook and improved results.

In order to get the best use out of this workbook, remember to date each new page that you use so that you can go back and easily manage your notes.

Finally, we wish you all the best in achieving that which you desire.

Good luck to you.

BE FOCUSSED. *Keep a daily To Do List.* Be **Productive** Every Minute. **ALWAYS WIN.** Keep Moving Forward.

All of my problems have a solution.

I am at Complete Ease

BE FOCUSSED. *Keep a daily To Do List.* Be **Productive** Every Minute. **ALWAYS WIN.** Keep Moving Forward.

All of my thoughts and feelings are under control.

I am Totally Relaxed

I am Totally Relaxed

I am totally relaxed

BE FOCUSSED. *Keep a daily To Do List.* Be **Productive** Every Minute. **ALWAYS WIN.** Keep Moving Forward.

All of my thoughts and feelings are under control.

I am in full control of my senses

I am in Full Control of my Senses

I am in full control of my senses

BE FOCUSSED. *Keep a daily To Do List.* Be **Productive** Every Minute. **ALWAYS WIN.** Keep Moving Forward.

All that I need comes to me at the right time and place in this life.

I Feel Alert and Ready

BE FOCUSSED. *Keep a daily To Do List.* Be **Productive** Every Minute. **ALWAYS WIN.** Keep Moving Forward.

Everything is good right now.

I Have the Wind in my Sails

BE FOCUSSED. *Keep a daily To Do List.* Be **Productive** Every Minute. **ALWAYS WIN.** Keep Moving Forward.

Everything works out for my highest good.

I can feel a strong force pushing me forward

I Can Feel a Strong Force Pushing me Forward

I can feel a strong force pushing me forward

BE FOCUSSED. *Keep a daily To Do List.* Be **Productive** Every Minute. **ALWAYS WIN.** Keep Moving Forward.

Following my intuition and my heart keeps me safe and sound.

I am a winner

I am a WINNER

I am a winner

BE FOCUSSED. *Keep a daily To Do List.* Be **Productive** Every Minute. **ALWAYS WIN.** Keep Moving Forward.

Giving up is easy and always an option so let's delay it for another day.

I Will Achieve Whatever I Visualize

BE FOCUSSED. *Keep a daily To Do List.* Be **Productive** Every Minute. **ALWAYS WIN.** Keep Moving Forward.

I accept and embrace all of life's experiences, even the unpleasant ones.

Each time I speak, I capture hearts and minds

Each Time I Speak, I Capture Hearts and Minds

Each time I speak, I capture hearts and minds

BE FOCUSSED. *Keep a daily To Do List.* Be **Productive** Every Minute. **ALWAYS WIN.** Keep Moving Forward.

I accept everyone as they are and continue on with pursuing my dream.

Success is Natural for me

BE FOCUSSED. *Keep a daily To Do List.* Be **Productive** Every Minute. **ALWAYS WIN.** Keep Moving Forward.

I accept responsibility if my anger has hurt anyone.

I am unaffected by the opinions of others

I am Unaffected by the Opinions of Others

I am unaffected by the opinions of others

BE FOCUSSED. *Keep a daily To Do List.* Be **Productive** Every Minute. **ALWAYS WIN.** Keep Moving Forward.

I adopt the mindset to praise myself.

I Embrace all and Fear None

BE FOCUSSED. *Keep a daily To Do List.* Be **Productive** Every Minute. **ALWAYS WIN.** Keep Moving Forward.

I am a better person from the hardship that I've gone through with my family.

Regardless of status, we all eat, breathe, sleep, defecate - we are ONE

(Fear Nobody)

Regardless of Status, we all eat, Breathe, Sleep, Defecate - we are ONE

Regardless of status, we all eat, breathe, sleep, defecate - we are ONE

BE FOCUSSED. *Keep a daily To Do List.* Be **Productive** Every Minute. **ALWAYS WIN.** Keep Moving Forward.

I am a good person at all times of day and night.

Welcome and accept every situation life offers you – it's there to improve you

Welcome and Accept Every Situation Life Offers You – it's There to Improve You

Welcome and accept every situation life offers you – it's there to improve you

BE FOCUSSED. *Keep a daily To Do List.* Be **Productive** Every Minute. **ALWAYS WIN.** Keep Moving Forward.

I am a magnet and I attract wealth and abundance.

Easy, Happy, Difficult, Harsh, Sad or Horrid – each life event will make you stronger

Easy, Happy, Difficult, Harsh, Sad or Horrid – Each Life Event Will Make You Stronger

Easy, Happy, Difficult, Harsh, Sad or Horrid – each life event will make you stronger

BE FOCUSSED. *Keep a daily To Do List.* Be **Productive** Every Minute. **ALWAYS WIN.** Keep Moving Forward.

I am a unique child of this world.

If you resist it – it will persist and bother you – submit to every situation in order to arrive at inner peace

If you Resist it – it will Persist and Bother you – Submit to Every Situation In Order to Arrive at Inner Peace

If you resist it – it will persist and bother you – submit to every situation in order to arrive at inner peace

BE FOCUSSED. *Keep a daily To Do List.* Be **Productive** Every Minute. **ALWAYS WIN.** Keep Moving Forward.

I am beautiful and smart and that's how everyone sees me.

Welcome the "NO" so you can get Closer to the "YES"

BE FOCUSSED. *Keep a daily To Do List.* Be **Productive** Every Minute. **ALWAYS WIN.** Keep Moving Forward.

I am completely in control of my thoughts.

Rejection is also a success because it is teaching you many lessons from which you grow

Rejection is also a Success; it is Teaching you many Lessons from which you Grow

Rejection is also a success because it is teaching you many lessons from which you grow

BE FOCUSSED. *Keep a daily To Do List.* Be **Productive** Every Minute. **ALWAYS WIN.** Keep Moving Forward.

I am deeply fulfilled with who I am.

I Continue to Seek New Knowledge and Experiences

BE FOCUSSED. *Keep a daily To Do List.* Be **Productive** Every Minute. **ALWAYS WIN.** Keep Moving Forward.

I am doing work that I enjoy and find fulfilling.

With every hurdle encountered I come closer to the result I am seeking

With Every Hurdle Encountered I Come Closer to the Result I am Seeking

With every hurdle encountered I come closer to the result I am seeking

BE FOCUSSED. *Keep a daily To Do List.* Be **Productive** Every Minute. **ALWAYS WIN.** Keep Moving Forward.

I am happy in my own skin and in my own circumstances.

Discovering wealth is easy and great fun

Discovering Wealth is Easy and Great Fun

Discovering Wealth is easy and great fun

BE FOCUSSED. *Keep a daily To Do List.* Be **Productive** Every Minute. **ALWAYS WIN.** Keep Moving Forward.

I am in complete charge of planning for my future.

I Enjoy my Profession

BE FOCUSSED. *Keep a daily To Do List.* Be **Productive** Every Minute. **ALWAYS WIN.** Keep Moving Forward.

I am more than good enough and I get better every day.

I grow as an individual with each day that passes

I Grow as an Individual with Each Day that Passes

I grow as an individual with each day that passes

BE FOCUSSED. *Keep a daily To Do List.* Be **Productive** Every Minute. **ALWAYS WIN.** Keep Moving Forward.

I am participating in the experiences of the moment.

I thrive on new challenges

I Thrive on New Challenges

I thrive on new challenges

BE FOCUSSED. *Keep a daily To Do List.* Be **Productive** Every Minute. **ALWAYS WIN.** Keep Moving Forward.

I am peacefully allowing my life to unfold.

I am Untouchable; I am the Best at What I do

BE FOCUSSED. *Keep a daily To Do List.* Be **Productive** Every Minute. **ALWAYS WIN.** Keep Moving Forward.

I am safe and sound. All is well.

Life is a challenge but I am ready for it

Life is a Challenge but I am Ready for it

Life is a challenge but I am ready for it

BE FOCUSSED. *Keep a daily To Do List.* Be **Productive** Every Minute. **ALWAYS WIN.** Keep Moving Forward.

I am thankful that I get to live another day.

Exceeding my targets is easy for me

Exceeding my Targets is Easy for me

Exceeding my targets is easy for me

BE FOCUSSED. *Keep a daily To Do List.* Be **Productive** Every Minute. **ALWAYS WIN.** Keep Moving Forward.

I am too big a gift to this world to feel self-pity.

I am the true master of my own destiny and I deserve the best

I am the True Master of my Own Destiny and I Deserve the Best

I am the true master of my own destiny and I deserve the best

BE FOCUSSED. *Keep a daily To Do List.* Be **Productive** Every Minute. **ALWAYS WIN.** Keep Moving Forward.

I answer questions about my dreams without getting defensive.

I sincerely love myself and believe that I can achieve REAL RESULTS

I Sincerely Love Myself and BELIEVE that I can Achieve REAL RESULTS

I sincerely love myself and believe that I can achieve REAL RESULTS

BE FOCUSSED. *Keep a daily To Do List.* Be **Productive** Every Minute. **ALWAYS WIN.** Keep Moving Forward.

I ask for and do meaningful, wonderful and rewarding work.

I am constantly present minded and centred within myself

I am Constantly Present Minded and Centred Within Myself

I am constantly present minded and centred within myself

BE FOCUSSED. *Keep a daily To Do List.* Be **Productive** Every Minute. **ALWAYS WIN.** Keep Moving Forward.

I ask my loved ones to support my dreams.

As I push myself, I become stronger

As I Push Myself, I Become Stronger

As I push myself, I become stronger

BE FOCUSSED. *Keep a daily To Do List.* Be **Productive** Every Minute. **ALWAYS WIN.** Keep Moving Forward.

I attempt all – not some – possible ways to get unstuck.

I have an impressive voice which creates a vortex of attraction

I Have an Impressive Voice which Creates a Vortex of Attraction

I have an impressive voice which creates a vortex of attraction

BE FOCUSSED. *Keep a daily To Do List.* Be **Productive** Every Minute. **ALWAYS WIN.** Keep Moving Forward.

I awake each day with excitement, awaiting the good things coming to me.

I am a huge success

I am a HUGE SUCCESS

I am a huge success

BE FOCUSSED. *Keep a daily To Do List.* Be **Productive** Every Minute. **ALWAYS WIN.** Keep Moving Forward.

I believe in my ability to change the world with the work that I do.

My Work Rate is Phenomenol;
I am Superior

BE FOCUSSED. *Keep a daily To Do List.* Be **Productive** Every Minute. **ALWAYS WIN.** Keep Moving Forward.

I believe in my ability to unlock the way and set myself free.

I am highly intelligent and articulate

I am Highly Intelligent and Articulate

BE FOCUSSED. *Keep a daily To Do List.* Be **Productive** Every Minute. **ALWAYS WIN.** Keep Moving Forward.

I breathe in and out, releasing all stress from my body.

I Overcome Objections with Empathy and Ease

BE FOCUSSED. *Keep a daily To Do List.* Be **Productive** Every Minute. **ALWAYS WIN.** Keep Moving Forward.

I breathe in calmness and breathe out nervousness.

I achieve ALL of my daily and weekly goals

I Achieve ALL of my Daily and Weekly Goals

I achieve ALL of my daily and weekly goals

BE FOCUSSED. *Keep a daily To Do List.* Be **Productive** Every Minute. **ALWAYS WIN.** Keep Moving Forward.

I cannot give up until I have tried every conceivable way.

My life is improving daily

My Life is Improving Daily

My life is improving daily

BE FOCUSSED. *Keep a daily To Do List.* Be **Productive** Every Minute. **ALWAYS WIN.** Keep Moving Forward.

I choose to find hopeful and optimistic ways to look at this.

I am able to create meaningful relationships with ease

I am Able to Create Meaningful Relationships with Ease

I am able to create meaningful relationships with ease

BE FOCUSSED. *Keep a daily To Do List.* Be **Productive** Every Minute. **ALWAYS WIN.** Keep Moving Forward.

I choose to fully participate in my day.

People approach me for guidance because they respect me

People Approach me for Guidance Because they Respect Me

People approach me for guidance because they respect me

BE FOCUSSED. *Keep a daily To Do List.* Be **Productive** Every Minute. **ALWAYS WIN.** Keep Moving Forward.

I choose to see my family as a gift.

I offer sincere advice, guidance and support to those in need of it

I Offer Sincere Advice, Guidance and Support to those in Need of it

I offer sincere advice, guidance and support to those in need of it

BE FOCUSSED. *Keep a daily To Do List.* Be **Productive** Every Minute. **ALWAYS WIN.** Keep Moving Forward.

I choose to see the light that I am to this world.

The more I help others, the more I am helping myself

The More I Help Others, the More I am Helping Myself

The more I help others, the more I am helping myself

BE FOCUSSED. *Keep a daily To Do List.* Be **Productive** Every Minute. **ALWAYS WIN.** Keep Moving Forward.

I compare myself only to my highest self.

I am able to overcome all challenges with great ease and enjoyment

I am Able to Overcome all Challenges with Great Ease and Enjoyment

I am able to overcome all challenges with great ease and enjoyment

BE FOCUSSED. *Keep a daily To Do List.* Be **Productive** Every Minute. **ALWAYS WIN.** Keep Moving Forward.

I draw from my inner strength and light.

I attract goodness through a powerful magnetic force field

I Attract Goodness Through a Powerful Magnetic Force Field

I attract goodness through a powerful magnetic force field

BE FOCUSSED. *Keep a daily To Do List.* Be **Productive** Every Minute. **ALWAYS WIN.** Keep Moving Forward.

I easily return to the present moment and what is happening to me.

Happiness Awaits me - I Simply Have to Accept it

BE FOCUSSED. *Keep a daily To Do List.* Be **Productive** Every Minute. **ALWAYS WIN.** Keep Moving Forward.

I embrace the peace and quiet of the night.

I Love my Life; I am Fulfilled, Successful and Growing

BE FOCUSSED. *Keep a daily To Do List.* Be **Productive** Every Minute. **ALWAYS WIN.** Keep Moving Forward.

I embrace the rhythm and the flowing of my own heart.

I Have Unlimited Energy;
I Keep Ploughing on

BE FOCUSSED. *Keep a daily To Do List.* Be **Productive** Every Minute. **ALWAYS WIN**. Keep Moving Forward.

I engage in work that impacts this world positively.

I am a problem solver and regularly have new ideas and strategies

I am a Problem Solver and Regularly Have New Ideas and Strategies

I am a problem solver and regularly have new ideas and strategies

BE FOCUSSED. *Keep a daily To Do List.* Be **Productive** Every Minute. **ALWAYS WIN.** Keep Moving Forward.

I feel the love of those who are not physically around me.

I am thankful to each individual that has contributed to making me who I am today

I am Thankful to each Individual that has Contributed to Making me who I am Today

I am thankful to each individual that has contributed to making me who I am today

BE FOCUSSED. *Keep a daily To Do List.* Be **Productive** Every Minute. **ALWAYS WIN.** Keep Moving Forward.

I fill my day with hope and face it with joy.

I Respect and Love Unconditionally

BE FOCUSSED. *Keep a daily To Do List.* Be **Productive** Every Minute. **ALWAYS WIN.** Keep Moving Forward.

I find joy in the moment.

My Focus is Powerful

My Focus is Powerful

My Focus is Powerful

BE FOCUSSED. *Keep a daily To Do List.* Be **Productive** Every Minute. **ALWAYS WIN.** Keep Moving Forward.

I focus on breathing and grounding myself.

I Always Achieve My Goals

BE FOCUSSED. *Keep a daily To Do List.* Be **Productive** Every Minute. **ALWAYS WIN.** Keep Moving Forward.

I follow my dreams no matter what.

I am humbled and truly appreciate each and every life event

I am Humbled and Truly Appreciate Each and Every Life Event

I am humbled and truly appreciate each and every life event

BE FOCUSSED. *Keep a daily To Do List.* Be **Productive** Every Minute. **ALWAYS WIN.** Keep Moving Forward.

I forgive myself for all the mistakes I have made.

BE FOCUSSED. *Keep a daily To Do List.* Be **Productive** Every Minute. **ALWAYS WIN.** Keep Moving Forward.

I forgive and love all.

My Diet is Constantly Improving for Better Health

My Diet is Constantly Improving for Better Health

My diet is constantly improving for better health

BE FOCUSSED. *Keep a daily To Do List.* Be **Productive** Every Minute. **ALWAYS WIN.** Keep Moving Forward.

I always achieve that which I visualize

BE FOCUSSED. *Keep a daily To Do List.* Be **Productive** Every Minute. **ALWAYS WIN.** Keep Moving Forward.

Whatever I visualize becomes reality

I am Robust and Adapt to all Situations

I am Robust and Adapt to all Situations

I am robust and adapt to all situations

BE FOCUSSED. *Keep a daily To Do List.* Be **Productive** Every Minute. **ALWAYS WIN.** Keep Moving Forward.

I am emotionally and mentally stable

BE FOCUSSED. *Keep a daily To Do List.* Be **Productive** Every Minute. **ALWAYS WIN.** Keep Moving Forward.

I have sincere love and care for myself - I look out for my best interests

I am Free and Happy

My Life is Complete

I am free and happy - my life is complete

BE FOCUSSED. *Keep a daily To Do List.* Be **Productive** Every Minute. **ALWAYS WIN.** Keep Moving Forward.

I am genuine, compassionate and caring

BE FOCUSSED. *Keep a daily To Do List.* Be **Productive** Every Minute. **ALWAYS WIN.** Keep Moving Forward.

I am Limitless

I take pride in everything I do

I Take Pride in
Everything I do

I take pride in everything I do

BE FOCUSSED. *Keep a daily To Do List.* Be **Productive** Every Minute. **ALWAYS WIN.** Keep Moving Forward.

I triple check everything. My attemtion to detail is high calibre

BE FOCUSSED. *Keep a daily To Do List.* Be **Productive** Every Minute. **ALWAYS WIN.** Keep Moving Forward.

I live a wholesome life

CPSIA information can be obtained
at www.ICGtesting.com
Printed in the USA
LVHW050914190119
604510LV00035B/579/P